Investment Strategies for Life

Walter E. Simmons III

Order this book online at www.trafford.com
or email orders@trafford.com

Most Trafford titles are also available at major online book retailers.

Printed in the United States of America.

ISBN: 978-1-4669-4773-3 (sc)
ISBN: 978-1-4669-4772-6 (hc)
ISBN: 978-1-4669-4774-0 (e)

Library of Congress Control Number: 2012912776

Trafford rev. 07/17/2012

 www.trafford.com

North America & international
toll-free: 1 888 232 4444 (USA & Canada)
phone: 250 383 6864 ♦ fax: 812 355 4082

Contents

Foreword

In this book, we will do what not a lot of authors have done in the financial world. We will give you examples of stocks to buy that fit your lifestyle and threshold. We will put forth different scenarios, which will help you pick the right stocks. We will give you choices as to the different portfolios that you should hold based on your situation. We will discuss some of the major sectors in those holdings. We will let you make choices on your own based on your tolerance of volatility of the market. We will discuss age and how that will affect you.

There is no such thing as a perfect portfolio; there is only a comfort level with it. No one knows your limits but you. Do you stay away from risk or do you embrace it? In my studies, I have found that risk is a necessary evil. A calculated risk is what I like to call it. Do not worry; I will always have the protection of your portfolio in mind.

My goal is to guide you through some of the major pitfalls of investing and to help you put together a portfolio that will make you relax and sleep well at night. I want to put all your fears aside and make you a powerful investor.

Can investing be safe? Yes, but not free of all risk. So make sure you understand your portfolio. An example to illustrate my point is if you live in a house and decided to get an alarm for safety. You are not free of all burglary risk. But you are safer and, therefore, more comfortable. So be an investor who is protected from most risk. Your portfolio is the same way; there are safeguards and protection that you can position in place that will put you at ease. This will be shown to you throughout this book.

You can become a great investor. Take your time and methodically go through this book. Use my book along with my insight into the stock market. Build your dream portfolio or use one of the ones that I am going to give you in this book to accomplish your financial goals. I want to teach you how to invest; what the proper steps to build a portfolio are; and illustrate, step by step, why you should buy certain stocks over others.

We will learn how to analyze and how to research a bunch of various stocks from different sectors through the meticulous research, which includes statistical analysis, studying of charts, listening to conference calls of your companies, and poring through major company SEC filings that have impacted the stock's daily volume or price positively or negatively. Learning how to correctly study and internalize these research methods is paramount. Think of this as having a thorough understanding of where your hard-earned money is going. Understand that this is your money at work. Do your due diligence.

We will discuss investment styles and trends of investors. We will discuss how a portfolio is broken down into capitalizations, sectors, and quality of stocks and making a decision that is thoughtful and comprehensive. A few different securities will be talked about throughout this text.

What Is This Book About?

In this book, I have written a series of essays on major topics in investing. These essays are written from my point of view and my understanding and views of how market has, is, and will function. People that are new to the stock market can and will follow this book's advice step by step. This should be used as a guide. For my more seasoned investors, this book can be used as a reference book and portfolio gauge.

This book is designed to be an easy read, a beginner and intermediate guide on to how to invest in the stock market. Unlike most investment books, I will pick stocks that I like and have done research on and show you, step-by-step, how to invest your money—even how to buy your stock directly—and I will help you break down the Wall Street gibberish and verbiage.

The purpose of this book is to give you information. No one teaches you what to do with your money, whether you're young or more mature. In the second grade, you are taught how to count money and add decimals, and then the next time you are introduced to money again is as a high school junior or senior in a semester-long elective if you're lucky. If and when you go to college—unless you're a finance, business, or economics major, or something related—you get to take another semester of learning about money and finances. And that's it. You basically get very little guidance when it comes to money at three very pivotal stages of your life. At seven, when you are at the stage where you can absorb the most, you are only exposed to money in the physical form. Once to get to be a seventeen or eighteen year old, you're probably working at a fast-food place part-time and have no idea how to do anything with your money but spend it. And finally in college, you're a broke student who is being bombarded with credit card offers and is wondering how to juggle tuition, apartment/rent money, books, repairs on that piece of junk you call a car, and let alone food. It's awful. You are equipped with all the skills you need, except for the one thing that can dictate your financial life. Your financial situation is what we will attack and improve with your money.

I will show you slowly and methodically how to put your money in the right places and have it work for you. I will describe the tricky terms used in the financial realm. I will successfully demonstrate ways to improve your chances of making money. I will compare and contrast investment styles and even give you some examples of actual portfolios. That's right, authentic portfolios and stocks to invest in. I will show how to be protective with your money and aggressive at the same time.

This is an easy and simple book. My hope is that you understand the basics of investing. I want you to know that you can do as well as the big players on Wall Street. With a little discipline, you can have high returns with your money in the market. No tricks, just an understanding of where you should put your money. If you figure out and learn what stocks fit your persona and gives you some form of gratification from owning them, by all means, go for it.

Some of the terms in this book may confuse you, this is not my intention. So as I introduce these terms, I will give you the definition of these terms. My goal is to enlighten you about all the opportunities that are included in becoming an investor.

This book is meant to be read in a matter of days, maybe two or three days maximum. It is a quick read and fast study. I want you to take the knowledge from this book and apply it right away.

Don't you want to read more about stocks? I find, as an avid investor, that it is difficult to find books that have authors that have picked stocks. These books are hard to find! Most people won't stick their necks out and recommend to you winning stocks from powerful portfolios.

I want you to stop what you are doing right now, and either write down your portfolio or get your portfolio statement. Ask yourself, how many stocks do you own? Are you diverse? How much dividend income do you have? And with this mix of stocks, you will meet your financial goals.

Fifty percent of all adult Americans are invested in the stock market in some form or fashion. Wow! Imagine how many people that is, 155 million out of the 311 million US citizens. Whether it's an individual investment account, hedge fund, or a retirement account, we are in it together! I hope you're ready to begin!

Background/Acknowledgments

I read *Wall Street Journal* every other day as well as the *Investor Business Daily* (IBD). I have also subscribed to *Motley Fool*'s newsletters. I also watch CNBC on a daily bases and have a bachelor of science in electrical engineering, a master of arts equivalence in mathematics. I also went to a very special and elite high school called Baltimore Polytechnic Institute. There, I got my foundation to learn and never stop learning. I would like to thank my family who always knew when to push me but never pushed too hard. I would also like to thank both sides of my family. To my three little girls, who are growing up so very fast, I love you. And finally, I would like to thank Mom and Dad, my ma for taking care of me all these years, and my dad for giving me my foundation for understanding investments and life. And to my sister whose toughness kept me strong. To my brother, make your own path in life and don't be afraid to fail. And lastly, to everyone who came into my life and even the ones who did not stay in my life. I would like to give you all a standing ovation.

Chapter 1

Your Foundation for Wealth
(Why is Investing Important?)

What's Important to You?

Everyone wants to be rich or well off. Whether you are born with it or you are struggling to get there. If you are born in America or another country that has free trade and enterprise, you have all the opportunity in the world to be successful and to get you a piece of the American pie, especially if you are investing.

It is important to invest for many reasons. The first reason is to invest for safety and financial security for you and your family. Providing for your family is one of the most important jobs that you will have during your lifetime. Invest to help yourself and your family. Another reason to invest is to have an income when you decide to retire. When you retire, you want to keep the same lifestyle you had when you were working. And some people tend to travel and vacation more in retirement, so make sure you build a good retirement nest egg. Invest for your children's college education. Your child deserves a college education, so while you are maximizing your retirement, put something aside for those little ones running around your legs. The next reason is so you can pass down wealth to your children and your children's children. Teaching your children about wealth and then putting that wealth in their hands is a very powerful act and will be a game changer for them and their children. My final reason, but this should not be your final one, is investing is important to you. That is right, you! You should invest for yourself. I always wanted a BMW, a luxury car that is quite expensive. One way to purchase it free and clear is to invest your money and let it grow. Or that dream house you always wanted, invest and pay cash with a down payment of 20 percent, half the value of the house or even the whole price of the house.

I had my first job, and I couldn't save a dime! Every month, I would go through my whole two paychecks. I paid my rent, food, car note, car insurance, hanging out, cable phone, cell phone, and parties. Until one day, I decided to invest fifty dollars a month in McDonald's (MCD), and after a small number of months, I put another fifty dollars in Duke Energy (DUK). Before you know it, you'll have a few thousands put away. This is something anybody can do, put away a few dollars a month and put youself on the path to wealth.

Does your family live paycheck to paycheck? Are you one paycheck from poverty? If you lost your job, would you be homeless in less than three months? Investing your money can change this. And if you truly care for your family, this step will give you the baseline to achieve security. By investing as little as fifty dollars a month through a brokerage firm or discount brokerage firm, you can change your life. Fifty dollars a month may seem like a lot, but check how much you paid for your cable last month and get back to me about not having any extra money. I started off building my future with fifty dollars a month with an oil company ExxonMobil (XOM). I started a few months after getting my first job in 2002. I invested in a direct purchase plan company called Computershare. I consistently put fifty dollars a month into this account and, sometimes, as much as a thousand dollars a month when I had a high tax return or a promotion at work. By doing this consistently, I amassed a large sum of money close to seventeen thousand dollars by 2005. You can do the exact the same thing through Computershare, with ExxonMobil (XOM), or some other stock company they offer. You can use this money to put a down payment of a house or buy a car.

During these times in 2012 when economic downturns are imminent, investing can be your key to your future. Our economic periods in the United States are cyclic in nature. Consistently investing over time can act as insulation to your investing future. We are going through a difficult time now; prepare yourself.

I beg you in these difficult times to invest. While the overall market and country is down with high unemployment, stocks like General Electric (GE), which have been beaten down during this downturn, are ripe for the picking, and must be bought especially if they pay a dividend. Blue chips that were vulnerable should be bought if the fundamentals are sound and ought to be held long term.

No financial institution wants you to read this book. The American dream is supposed to be dead. You are supposed to be in credit card debt and upside down on your house and car note. You are supposed to work several different jobs in a lifetime; you're not as privileged as your father or grandfather to get a pension from working the same job for thirty-six years. You are supposed to spend uncontrollably and leverage yourself to your eyeballs.

You will not get a pension, so you better learn to invest. If you're working now, you are likely to have a 401K that is matched in some form or fashion. With a 401K, your retirement is what you make it. What you put in is what you get out. It is all up to you now.

What Is a Stock?

Stock = Ownership

Stock is a fraction of the ownership of a usually publicly traded company. If you own stock, you are called a shareholder. Ownership is the cornerstone of life. If you own stock, you own a piece of a company. The more stock you purchase, the more equity you build up in the company of your choice.

Stock, which can be represented by a stock certificate, entitles you to a portion of the profits and assets, or both, of the institution on paper, and this paper gives you ownership of profits and voting privileges on matters concerning the company. These profits are usually paid out in the form of dividends.

Stock certificates can be requested from your brokerage accounts. The certificate is mainly just a physical representation of the company and the number of shares you own. I recommend that you do not keep high-valued stock certificates in your home. Would you leave a large sum of money in your home?

An Old Investing Rule!

In investing there is an old rule for the percentage of stock you should own in your portfolio: the number 110 minus your age is the amount that you should own in stocks. A quick example of this is a twenty-eight-year-old wanting to know how much stock to own. So to get her percentage of stock that she should own, you take $110 - 28 = 82$. She should own 82 percent in stock and 18 percent in bonds within her portfolio. The newer rule calls for 125 minus your age. This new theory is in place because people are living longer into their eighties and even their nineties. A little more risk in your portfolio is needed because your money will be expected to last longer. This is the new portion of your portfolio that ought to be in stock. There is another rule that I go by, it states that you should be in all stock until you reach the age of 30, and as you get older, you should add a percentage of bonds. For example, a person aged 35 should have 5 percent in bonds and 95 percent of your investable money in stocks. This rule applies up to fifty-fifty stock to bond ratio. I also believe you should keep 50 percent stock in your portfolio as long as the stocks pay a dividend even if you're seventy-five years old or older. Basically, I believe you should be in stocks in some form or fashion your entire life.

Rule 72 and Compounding

Rule 72 or sometimes called Rule of 72 is a technique for figuring out the estimating time of an investment doubling. For example, if you were to invested $500 with compounding interest at 5 percent yearly, Rule 72 states 72/5 = 14.4 years required for the investment to double and be worth $1,000. This is not a math trick, as some people may say, but a basic math computation that is closer to an approximation.

Compounding is earnings reinvested in order to generate their own earnings or more commonly thought of as making interest on interest. Compounding also can be stated as the addition of interest to the principal so that the interest added also earns interest and continuous until it is withdrawn or interrupted. When your money first starts to compound, it may seem small or modest, but if you stick with it year after year, your returns will accelerate exponentially assuming an average return of 7-10 percent return annually. Compounding can help you with the pesky problem of inflation eating at your portfolio's value. Regularly contributing to your portfolio through cash purchase of stocks makes your portfolio compound quickly.

A Hundred Shares or Round Lots

As a small investor, you may not be able to afford to buy 100 or 200 shares of a certain stock. If you buy a 100 or 200 or any multiple of hundred, you will be buying what is called a round lot. I feel that it is not necessary to buy a round lot if you can't afford them. It is okay to buy 10 or 25 shares if that is all you can afford at that time. It doesn't matter how many shares you purchase at first, if you've done the research; it's okay to purchase stock that are 200 dollars, 300 dollars, 400 dollars, 500 dollars, or higher a share. It's okay to buy 25 shares of Apple (APPL) to start a position or 35 shares of MasterCard (MA) at 400 plus dollars a share. I want you in these well-performing stocks; I don't care how expensive their price looks. I am more concerned with how strong their fundamentals and earnings are. You should build your position over time in these great stocks—25 shares here, 25 shares there. It all adds up. Just please get in!

Why Own Stock?

Investing is a joy for me. I love to invest. Investing should be done for enjoyment, for the fun of ownership, and to help you get to retirement. Don't make investing a second job. It should be done for enjoyment. Let's briefly look at other investments.

Cash loses its purchasing power over time because of inflation. So being in all cash hurts you over time.
Bonds will give you 2-4 percent return on your money.
Gold is very volatile but, over the past few years, has come on strong in returns.
Stocks will return usually anywhere from 7-11 percent annually with dividends that percentage will explode higher.

Ticker Symbols

Each stock discussed in this book will have its ticker symbol next to it in parentheses. What is a ticker symbol? You may be asking. A ticker symbol is an alphabetical series of letters that represent a given company. Heinz's, ticker symbol is (HNZ). This is an example.

Strategy No. 1: Buying on Splits

One of my favorite strategies when I first started investing was buying right before stocks split or right after they split. I understand that when a stock splits, the monetary value of the stock is the same. Make sure you buy on common stock splits that pay a dividend of some sort. A dividend is like an umbrella of protection. So when investing, make sure you're under it.

There are companies that do not like when their share price gets too high, so they split their stock to make their share price more attractive to investors.

Before a stock split, there is a period of stock appreciation up until the stock splits. If the stock market is in an upward trend, you can reap these benefits before and after the announcement. Good research will help you figure out who is an outstanding split candidate. Read as much financial news as you can stand. That includes magazines, internet, newspapers, and newsletters. Once you have found a couple of candidates. Dig your teeth into them and bite down like it's a juicy T-bone steak, side of potatoes, and garden salad.

After a stock split, it is a great time to get a stock at an inexpensive price. It may rise a few points, and then it usually trades in a range dropping then rising and dropping then rising for a few quarters. Don't be alarmed; this is normal that a stock trades in this type of tight trading pattern. What is a stock split? A stock split is usually when a stock's shares double, but its price is halved.

There are companies that do not like when their share price gets to high, so they split their stock to make their share price more attractive to investors.

StrategyNo. 2: Breakups and Spin-Offs

Companies buy each other all the time. The big fish gobbles up the small fish and keeps adding companies or swallowing up smaller fish. Look out! When the big fish gets too big, it's usually time for a breakup to unleash the company's hidden value. If the two separate companies are worth more than the whole, usually the company is split or broken up. Do not confuse the word stock split with company split or break up. A stock split, remember, is when the shares are usually split or the common stock is doubled 2:1, 3:2 (for every three shares, you get two more), or 4:3 (for every four shares you have, you get three more). So do not confuse them.

Buying when it is announced that a company is breaking up is ideal. (1) Normally, the stock will rise in value from the time of the announcement until the actual breakup. (2) For the most part, two companies are better than one, and finally (3) if both companies will pay dividends. Examples of this are Abbott Labs (ABT) and Kraft (KFT) that by all means should be purchased ahead of time before breakup.

Spin-offs are when the company remains intact and a piece of the parent company becomes its own standalone company. One such company that has done this of recent years is Altria

(MO), spinning off companies of the likes of Kraft (KFT) and Phillip Morris International (PM).

Joel Greenblatt, in his book, *You Can Be a Stock Market Genius*, describes the purpose of a spin-off. He states, "Spinoffs can take many forms, but the end result is usually the same: A corporation takes a subsidiary division or part of its business and separates it from the parent company by creating a new, independent free-standing company."

I recommend buying the parent company before it spins off any parts of its business. And please get in early. The earlier you buy, the better off you are because in most instances, the company will announce about a year or more in advance that they will be spinning off a section of their business. So after you have done your homework, jump in with both feet. This allows the stock price to go up because the company usually does not have two companies priced into its stock price. In most cases, it only has the value of one, giving you a year of momentum before the spin-off. In most cases, there is another pop when the spin-off IPOs and is given to shareholders of the parent company.

What Gives You the Right?

What gives me the right to write this book? What are your credentials?

I am not an insider. I am not a high-flying investor. I am not a Wall Street guru. I am a regular guy who works every day, making $45,000 a year. I am not a CNBC analyst making millions. What I am is someone who has an engineering and mathematics background in industry and academia. I have been successful in investing long term, and I want to give you the skills and knowledge to make rational investing decisions in any financial climate.

I only want to see you successful in the future. I want you to reach your goals financially and otherwise. I want to guide you through the stock market with sound intelligent investment strategies.

What Every Investor Should Know?

Stocks are risky; it does not matter what kind of stock you own. When investing in a stock, it can do one of two things: go up or down. No stock stays where it is, contrary to what some people think and say.

If you invest money in "good" stocks over a five- to ten-year period, you should expect 7-10 percent return annually; with dividends, it is 2-5 percent more.

Find your comfort level with stocks. I will help you find that level, if needed. I will hold your hand and walk you through the progression of building a portfolio that you and your family can live with. I will give you a step-by-step breakdown of sectors, portfolios, and even a few stocks that will give you confidence to going forward with portfolios that you can enjoy and have assurance in.

Some Winning Quotes

In the *Wall Street Journal* (WSJ) is a quote, "Long-term portfolios are going to have short term volatility." This makes very good sense because the longer you hold stocks, the less severe upward and downward swings you will incur in your portfolio.

In thinking long term, IBD in Monday, June 28, 2010 special report states, "that investing in small-cap and large-cap stocks if you invest $10,000 per year it will take 22 and 23 years respectively to grow to a million." Now let's analyze this. Small caps should greatly improve your portfolio, yet it only gives you a one-year lead on large cap; this reinforces that large caps should be at your core, with large cap returning 11.23 percent annually, and small cap returning 12.23 percent yearly average rate of return. Large-cap stocks normally pay a dividend, making them less risky and a hedge against inflation and a saving account.

Albert Einstein states, "The power of compounding was said to be deemed the eighth wonder of the world."

Chapter 2

Your Nucleus of Your Portfolio
(What Stocks You Should Hold)

The Ideal Portfolio

When you begin investing, your portfolio ought to consist of ten common blue-chip stocks that pay dividends. Why? Blue chips are the cornerstone of your assortment of stocks, and you want well-known and high-producing cash flow companies within to start out. In addition to that, you should have two to three small cap stocks preferably that pay a dividend as well, but this is highly unlikely. Finally, two to three initial public offering (IPO) stocks that have gone public recently.

You want blue-chip stocks for consistence of your portfolio. These stocks are not volatile. This means that the stocks do not jump very often up or down, so these stocks must be held and not traded. The small cap stocks give your portfolio growth. IPOs can greatly increase your wealth, but you have to be responsible. Do not ever put money into an IPO that you have not put in time to do research in; that includes going through the companies' S-1. An S-1 is the company's filing paperwork to disclose potent information about the company and its future IPO filing. Research your stock picks: two examples of IPOs that I brought were MasterCard (MA) and Mead Johnson Nutrition (MJN). Both were no-brainers! I recommended a third to a person close to me at its IPO. That stock was Visa (V). You want to practice timing the market with IPOs. I personally wait three to four months and sometimes as long as eight months to buy. I keep track of institutional ownership especially after the usually sixth-month release of stock where prior IPO shareholders can sell their shares. You can keep track of this ownership through Google or Yahoo financial sites. I use these tools daily. As far as the volatility of these stocks, it can be tough to stomach at times. I know when the Senate passed the credit card regulations on May 14, 2010, MasterCard (MA) dropped 19.86. I said to myself yikes, but remembered how it had started paying a dividend. The stock dropped from an open of 232.31 and fell to 212.45 at close. The bigger and better the IPO, the more likely they are to pay a dividend eventually. All the companies that I have mentioned have a strong and reputable balance sheet and image. So having children and using a product like Enfamil, which is a great seller for Mead Johnson Nutrition (MJN), I bought it at IPO with no reservation. Mead Johnson Nutrition (MJN) is also a spin-off of Bristol-Myers Squibb (BMY). We will have more about this in a later chapter of this book.

Why Own Stocks?

If you could own any financial investment over the last fifty years including gold, bonds, CDs, cash, or stocks, which would you choose? Even though gold has had a hell of a run the past few years, over the long term, dividend paying blue-chip stock have far outpaced all others combined.

Chances are, if you pick the right blue-chip dividend-paying stock and hold it for over forty to fifty years. You should have a nice financial cushion after that time. A couple of examples are Proctor & Gamble (PG), General Electric (GE), and Altria (MO). With Proctor & Gamble (PG), you would have over a million; with Altria (MO), you would have about 2.1 million dollars; and finally, with General Electric (GE), you would have about 500,000 dollars.

Gold has had a great run over the past few years; I don't think the move is sustainable over the long haul. Also, gold does not pay a dividend. But something that I do like is a gold stock, which pays one. More in a second.

Strategy No. 3: Gold Stocks

So you want to invest in gold. You say it has had a huge upside run, and you want in. Thinking about a gold mutual fund? Think again. Buy a gold stock with a dividend. Gold has been aggressively moving to the upside. A gold stock will give you more diversification. A gold stock is a security that mirrors or trades near the price of gold usually but sometimes can trade well above or well below the price of gold. Goldcorp (GG) has been one of the best performing gold stocks to own. This is the best of the best gold stock. Goldcorp (GG) pays a 1 percent dividend. Another gold stock is Randgold Resources Limited (GOLD). I like this one as well.

Strategy No. 4: Blue Chips

In your portfolio, there are major stocks that you should hold. These stocks are called blue chips. Most of these stocks are Fortune 500 companies such as Wal-Mart (WM), Disney (DIS), McDonald's (MCD), and Pepsi (PEP) to name a few. You want these stocks to be heavily weighted in your portfolio. Why? Well, mainly because you want to keep 15-20 of these stocks in your portfolio. Your portfolio should consist of 30-35 stocks total. Another reason for you to hold blue chips is that the market value does not fluctuate or change very much. Also, almost all of these stocks pay a dividend. So you will get paid while you wait for the value of the stock to increase.

In my core portfolio, I hold Pfizer (PFE), Caterpillar (CAT), Duke Energy (DUK), AT&T (T), Coca-Cola (KO), and ExxonMobil (XOM). You want to be diversified. Diversification is the key to a strong portfolio. In your portfolio, you should have a core of stocks that pay a dividend, along with a few international and small cap stocks. Also, you should put in a small amount of money into initial public offerings (IPOs). But we will talk about that in a later chapter. Blue-chip stocks are the best and the brightest stock. They are what most institutions and individual investors buy. And you should do the same.

The Standard and Poor's (S&P) 500 is a large capital index of American companies. And that's where the majority of your money should go, into stocks in those companies. Blue chips that are well run generally return 7-13 percent annually.

Strategy No. 5:   Buy What You Own!

You should invest in companies whose products are in your house. In other words, buy stock in what you own and what you purchase on a regular basis. I don't just mean what's in your house. What do you purchase outside of the house? Everything from healthcare products, computers, software, foods, beverages, refrigerators, washing machines, television set, cable providers, and your favorite channels you like to watch. Don't know which stocks to buy? Start with companies that make these products. Look on the back of popular products in your favorite grocery store on its shelves. Take a drive and count the number of your favorite fast-food chain and regular restaurants that are in your hometown area on one lazy Sunday afternoon. Later, when you get home, match them up with their parent company to see if they are publicly traded. It's easy to do. Buy what you own!

Strategy No. 6: Master-Limited Partnership and Preferred Stock

It is okay to own master-limited partnerships in the form of stocks. They usually carry a high yield. When you own these limited partnerships, you are only responsible for the amount that you invested. You cannot be liable for other unlawful damages that your company may incur. They are a great investment to hold, and I recommend them in your portfolio.

Buckeye Partners (BPL) is a master-limited partnership that I advocate. It pays a hefty 6 percent dividend.

Preferred stock is another form of investment that is above common stock. Preferred stock has no voting privileges, and its dividends are distributed before the common shareholders get theirs. Basically, they have priority over common stock shareholders. In the event of a bankruptcy, assets are divided first among preferred shareholders.

Strategy No. 7: Real Estate Investment Trusts (REITS)

REITS, also called real estate investment trusts, are very good investment opportunities. REITS are required to distribute 90 percent of their earnings in the form of dividends. As long as the firms are profitable and earning at more than three times the dividend multiple (three times the quarterly dividend), they are okay to invest in. This is great for income investors and is a good source of dividends and cash flow to a portfolio. REITS should be held in individual accounts and not IRAs because of tax implications.

One of my favorite is Annaly Capital Management (NLY), which invests in real estate assets that are backed by the federal government. These stocks can be considered risky if earning falters. It yields around 13 percent.

Small Capitalization (Cap) Stocks

Small capital stocks are formally known as small market capitalization this means companies with a market cap of between $300 million to $2 billion. Small cap stocks are a second tier of investment that is behind large cap. I recommend small cap stocks to a lesser degree than large cap. Why? This is because small cap companies are producing less revenue and profits. In difficult times, people shy away from small cap for more stable large cap stocks.

You should have small capital stocks in the nucleus of your portfolio. There should be anywhere from 5 to 10 stocks in your portfolio. I already know what you're going to say. Those stocks are volatile, they are risky, and they may fail. And the answers are yes, yes, and yes. These statements all can be true. When large caps are struggling look to these stocks to lead the way in the investment world; if you have good fortune, you may find some small caps that pay a modest dividend. Consider it the best of both worlds.

But do not keep yourself from big gains by shying away from this type of stock because of a little volatility. Remember, do your research and buy quality small cap with a high-quality business model, strong earnings, and superior fundamentals.

Mutual Funds

"I like my mutual funds, they are safe and are pretty effective as an investment option. Why should I buy stocks? My mutual fund pays a 3 percent dividend and has decent growth."

Well, to begin, you're absolutely right: mutual funds are safe investments. They are the right investment, if you don't want to do research and analyze stocks.

What is a mutual fund? But why invest in a mutual fund? A mutual fund is a large group of stocks regularly made up of individual stocks frequently in the same sector but sometimes diversified over many sectors. A mutual fund is a design to track the performance of a sector or capitalization typically. They can also be a mixture of stocks along many different sectors and/or capitalizations. Why not get all the money and dividends that you have coming to you with just a tad more risk. Buy stocks over mutual funds, if you are comfortable doing so, and reap greater rewards. Instead of getting maybe 2 or 3 percent dividend on your money with mutual funds, get stocks paying as much and more than twice as much of a dividend on each individual stock.

CEOs

Philip Fisher states in *The People Factor*, "The company with real investment merit is the company that usually promotes from within . . . . A large company's need to bring in a new chief executive from the outside is a damning sign of something basically wrong with the existing management."

This is a very powerful statement by Mr. Fisher that companies that promote from within show how strong and profitable they are. The talent is in your own organization, which means you have recruited, hired, trained, and mentored intelligent individuals whom you have groomed and nurtured to take over any position one or two steps above their current one. Bringing in a new CEO from an outside organization throws a red flag to investors and shows the world that the company does not have a good line of succession in place.

As an investor, this all falls under research. Study your CEO of the stock company. How is he or she performing? Is there a likely person waiting in the wings to take over and succeed the top management positions?

Strategy No. 8: Thirty Stocks to Wealth

How should you study, analyze, and make the most of your portfolio of thirty stocks? Well, that depends on what you hold. For blue-chip stocks, once-a-month research will be good enough. For IPOs, twice a week of research may be necessary. Small cap once a week should be your minimum. If you own volatile movers, you want to check Google or Yahoo finance websites for information daily. I would also advise reading newspapers like *Barron's*, *WSJ*, and *IBD*, giving you info on the market daily and weekly. They are great sources of information and market knowledge.

Aren't thirty too many stocks? Yes, thirty is too many. I came up with the number 30 because there are ten sectors; you should hold at least three stocks in each sector, giving you thirty different stocks. Also to get to almost perfect diversification or 100 percent expansion, thirty is the number without getting redundant. The key to owning this many stocks is to know what is going on with each sector at any given time. Some examples, big snowstorm in the northeast. How are utilities performing? Oil spiked again. How is the energy market doing? Mortgage crisis. How about what's happening in the financial sector? If you understand your sectors, I guarantee you will know what's going on with your stock.

So what should your ideal portfolio look like? It should be one of these three portfolios or a variation of one listed below:

A. Medium Risk
   15 blue chips
   10 small caps
   5 IPOs

B. Ideal Conservative
   20 blue chips
   5 small caps
   5 IPOs

C. Aggressive Risk
   10 blue chips
   10 small caps
   10 IPOs

In addition to the previous layouts of portfolios, I will give you a stock-by-stock breakdown of the medium risk portfolio (A).

The medium risk portfolio will give you a balance between conservative and aggressive. It has risk but with 15 blue chips to smooth things out and give you some dividends. I have held this type of portfolio throughout my investment career.

PORTFOLIO A

15 blue chips—McDonald's (MCD), Amazon (AMZN), Coca-Cola (KO), Wal-Mart (WM), Pfizer (PFE), ExxonMobil (XOM), Wells Fargo (WFC), Johnson & Johnson (JNJ), General Electric (GE), Union Pacific (UNP), Newmont Mining (NEM), Apple (APPL), AT&T (T), Southern (SO), Duke Energy (DUK)

10 small caps—CF Industries Holdings (CF), Novo Nordisk (NVO), Red Robin Gourmet Burgers (RRBG), Royal Gold (RGLD), Panera Bread (PNRA), BioMarin Pharmaceutical

(BMRN), First Niagara Financial Group (FNFG), West Energy (WR), ITC Holdings (ITC), Strum, Ruger & Company (RGR)

5 IPOs—MasterCard (MA), Visa (V), Dunkin' Donuts (DNKN), Domino's Pizza (DPZ), Mead Johnson Nutrition (MJN)

This is just one example of what a powerful Simmons portfolio will look like. Also to note, this is moderate or medium risk portfolio, which is loaded with dividends.

In addition to the previous layouts of portfolio, I will give you a stock-by-stock breakdown of the conservative ideal portfolio (B).

The ideal conservative portfolio is a low-risk portfolio with high-yielding dividend plays. Ultraconservative plays on stocks that will help you sleep well. Be well assured this assortment of stocks will let you snooze at night.

PORTFOLIO B

20 blue chips—McDonald's (MCD), Walt Disney (DIS), Philip Morris International (PM), Kraft Foods (KFT), Altria Group (MO), Pepsi (PEP), Pfizer (PFE), Abbott Labs, ExxonMobil (XOM), General Electric (GE), Verizon Communications (VZ), Duke Energy (DUK), Dominion Resources (D), International Business Machines (IBM), Microsoft (MSFT), DuPont(DD), Monsanto (MON), ConocoPhillips (COP), JP Morgan (JPM), United Technologies (UTX)

5 small caps—CF Industries Holdings (CF), Novo Nordisk (NVO), Red Robin Gourmet Burgers (RRGB), Royal Gold (RGLD), Panera Bread (PNRA)

5 IPOs—MasterCard (MA), Visa (V), Dunkin' Donuts (DNKN), Domino's Pizza (DPZ), Mead Johnson Nutrition (MJN)

This is just one example of what a powerful Simmons portfolio will look like. Also to note, this is conservative-defensive portfolio, which is loaded with dividends.

My stock-by-stock breakdown of the aggressive ideal portfolio (C) is shown below.

The aggressive risk portfolio is a very intense, heart-pounding, jump on the wild side. As much risk as you can stand without becoming unbalanced or undiversified. This has a high level of risk in a portfolio.

PORTFOLIO C

10 blue chips—McDonald's (MCD), ExxonMobil (XOM), General Electric (GE), Verizon Communications (VZ), Dominion Resources (D), Berkshire Hathaway B (BRK.B), Johnson & Johnson (JNJ), Proctor & Gamble (PG), Apple(APPL), DuPont (DD)

10 small caps—CF Industries Holdings (CF), Novo Nordisk (NVO), Red Robin Gourmet Burgers (RRGB), Royal Gold (RGLD), Panera Bread (PNRA), BioMarin Pharmaceutical (BMRN), First Niagara Financial Group (FNFG), West Energy (WR), ITC Holdings (ITC), Strum, Ruger & Company (RGR)

10 IPOs—Mastercard (MA), Visa (V), Dunkin' Donuts (DNKN), Domino's Pizza (DPZ), Mead Johnson Nutrition (MJN), Facebook (FB), Phillip Morris International (PM), Caesars Entertainment (CZR), InvenSense (INVN), Lululemon Athletica (LULU)

Another example of Simmons portfolio, this is an aggressive portfolio.

I have just showed you three portfolios or three assortments of stocks styles. This selection of stocks that I have given to you are for balance. I have also tried to give you three levels of portfolios that are not overly conservative or aggressive.

What made me design a portfolio like this? To give you alternatives to the boring and unbalanced portfolio that you and I have run across. You want a challenging group of stocks that will keep your attention. These portfolios and stocks will put you on the road to wealth.

What makes your portfolio better than my financial advisor? Well, first of all, I am not going to force you into some ultra age-guided, conservative mutual fund that you contribute your hard-earned money into while taking a 1-2 percent commission of your money yearly. And second, I'm not going to give you all blue chips all the time and call it a day while pitching you life insurance.

Please keep in mind that portfolios do and will need to be updated and adjusted. Depending on your comfort level, the more aggressive the portfolio, the more research needs to be done. The more established and larger cap companies, the less research that needs to be done. I am not saying slack on your research because you will always need to watch earnings, make sure the company has rising or profitable earnings that are making money for the institution and you as well.

Chapter 3

Holding Certain Stocks with Dividends

Strategy No. 9: Dividends

A dividend is a return on a shareholder's investment usually in the form of cash or stock. Okay, well, how are dividend payments established? The record dates ascertain which shareholders of record will receive the dividend on that date. The ex-dividend date is the four business days prior to the date. The ex-dividend date institutes who is entitled to the dividend. The payment date is the date when the firm payouts cash dividends to shareholders.

Dr. Jeremy J. Siegel states, "Historically, value stocks—those with lower P/E ratios and higher dividend yields—have superior returns and lower risk than growth stocks" (362). Value stocks are usually low priced, high dividend yielding, and have strong fundamentals. The investor sees this stock as undervalued or a bargain. The investor usually purchases shares before the price of the shares goes back to the normal or suggested price. P/E ratios could be in the single digits or low teens.

So can dividends be compounded, and how can they improve my portfolio exponentially? Well, dividends are profits shared by companies with shareholders. That can be paid out in cash and can be reinvested and compounded usually quarterly (every four months). So, imagine if this were happening with several stocks and you're receiving dividends, over the years, this can greatly improve your overall portfolio year after year.

Dividends are crucial to any successful portfolio. Dividends can be used as an income source for those in retirement. But if they are reinvested, they can have you on the way to financial freedom. Appreciation, along with dividends, will make stocks even more valuable. Basically, your stock grows at a certain rate, and every quarter you get more shares. That means every four months, you get cash, which is used to purchase more shares for more stable companies that are growing the dividend and whose stock is rising as well for the most part.

Dividend yield is just the percentage of dividends you receive from the shareholder's parent company.

Ten Major Sectors

There are ten major sectors in the investment world. They are (1) utilities, (2) consumer staples industrials, (3) consumer discretionary, (4) healthcare, (5) financial, (6) telecommunication services, (7) materials, (8) industrials, (9) energy, and (10) technology. These sectors should be represented in the nucleus of your portfolio. We will talk about how they should be weighted now. The term *weighted* just means how much stock you own within each sector and, within the sector, what percentage of that sector's stock you have. This may seem a little confusing, so I'll give you an example. In the healthcare sector, say you choose 3 stocks: Pfizer (PFE), Merck (MRK), and Bristol-Myers (BMY). You buy a breakdown of 300 shares Pfizer, 200 Merck shares, and 50 Bristol-Myers shares. So you have 550 total shares healthcare stocks. You have 300/550, which is your Pfizer (PFE) position divided by the total number of healthcare shares. Doing the simple math, Pfizer equals 0.545 = 54.5 percent of your healthcare stock. Next doing the math, 200/550 would give you 0.364 = 36.4 percent of Merck in your healthcare sector. Finally, you have 50/550, which equals 0.091 = 9.1 percent and remaining percentage of your healthcare part. The percentage added up will give you 100 percent. You can also find the overall weight of your portfolio by doing similar easy calculations or basic fifth grade mathematics. So do not get intimidated.

Jeremy J. Siegel intelligently says, "Philip Morris is not the only firm that has served investors well. The return on the other 19 best-performing surviving companies has beaten the return on the S&P 500 Index by between 3 and 5 percent per year. Of the top 20 firms, 16 are dominated by two industries; consumer staples, represented by internationally well known consumer brand—name companies, and healthcare, particularly large pharmaceutical firms" (61). Dr. Siegel highlights in his book consumer staples and healthcare sector stocks from the S&P between the years 1957 through 2006 that have returned 14-19 percent annually over those 49 years. Some of these companies include some of my favorites like Altria (MO), Abbott Labs (ABT), Merck (MRK), Pepsico (PEP), Coca-Cola (KO), Pfizer (PFE), Proctor & Gamble (PG), and Hershey's (HSY) are a few from that list.

Yes, these are stocks with great past performance. So you might be saying or thinking past performance does not mean future gains. I would say yes, that is correct; it does not, but almost 50 years of great performance is an awfully long time to ignore such a superior feat especially if consistence, a dividend, and 14 percent returns are what you are looking for in a stock. Consumer staples and healthcare are where you begin to build your portfolio. These 14 percent plus annualized returns are produced with the help of all reinvested dividends.

I hold many of these stocks in my portfolio, and I recommend you do the same.

I will discuss each sector and give you my views. Let me warn you that sectors are and can be very cyclical.

Utilities

Some of the most dominating dividend-producing stocks are utilities. Southern (SO), Dominion Resources (D), Exelon (EXC), Duke Energy (DUK), Consolidated Edison (ED) are a few powerhouse utility companies that can be played in any portfolio and will give you a dividend ranging from 3.5 percent to 5 percent yield.

Consumer Staples

Your nucleus of your stock holdings requires you to include consumer staples and discretionary stocks. Consumer staples stocks consist of Kraft (KFT), Kellogg's (K), General Mills (GIS), Pepsi (PEP), and Coca-Cola (KO), to name a few. These stocks, for the most part, are foods and drinks found in your supermarket. You buy these products because you like them, which give way to such things as brand loyalty. Other family members like them such as kids. You make breakfast food in the morning when you are in a rush, like cold or hot cereal and orange juice. Still yet, others use cheeses. Some of these companies make snack foods for the Super Bowl or National Championship Games. They make snacks like chips and soda for fun times. Regardless of when or what you are buying, these staples have been and will continue to be purchased. In a down economy, do you think a mother will tell her children that they cannot have their favorite cereal or bag of chips go with their lunch. What is more likely is that the parents cannot afford for the child to buy lunch at school every day, so they pack a Kraft's (KFT) cheese and turkey sandwich, Pepsi's (PEP) Doritos, a piece of fruit, and a bottle of Aquafina water by Coca-Cola (KO). Even in a recession, folks, this happens every day. These companies dominate our pockets, and they will turn your investment to huge profits over time.

I took a psychology course in college, and the psyche of a human always fascinated me. Also, I heard a lot growing up that this is a consumer-based society. How many times did you hear that in your economics class? If you take these two concepts and bring them together, think how I can make money off this knowledge in the stock market. If they like a product or need a product, i.e. food to survive, then they will come back for the same product that they enjoyed over and over again.

Another powerful member of the consumer staples sector is tobacco. And love it or hate it, it is loaded with profits for you and your portfolio. One company has specially dominated the investment world. That name is Altria; if you would have bought this company fifty years ago under a different name and would have just held the stock, you would be a multimillionaire. The company in the last ten years has broken itself up into several other companies, all profitable and with good dividends.

Disclaimer: I understand the moral complexities of buying a tobacco or alcohol stock. I feel that it is an individual's decision whether to be an owner of these types of stocks. More later on this subject.

Consumer Discretionary

Consumer discretionary is the next sector I want to talk about. These sectors consist of companies like McDonald's (MCD), Yum Brands (YUM), Disney (DIS), and Wal-Mart (WM). This sector, unlike consumer staples, is more about wants than needs. As a kid, I always wanted to go to McDonald's for their golden french fries and Happy Meal toys. This was a treat for most kids growing up. Or how about this one, a trip to Disney

World or Disneyland is almost like a rite of passage nowadays. A parent has to take their child to Disney amusement parks before their sixteenth birthday. It is an unspoken rule among parents. For me, it was Disney World. Or ladies, I have one for you; tell your husband and children that you're canceling the cable TV. That's right, no ESPN for your husband and no Disney Channel for the kids. Again, investing in this sector is about wants.

Healthcare

The healthcare or medical sector is one of the ten major sectors. I highlight healthcare because it is a game changer based on the demographics of the baby boomers population turning sixty-five as a group over the next five years. Medicines, surgeries, procedures, and other medical products will be needed by these senior citizens in droves.

Some people may say, "Wait a second! What about universal healthcare? What about free healthcare for all? Won't this destroy healthcare stocks and the industry as a whole? Making everything free for all people, citizens or not."

I believe that yes, minor procedures and doctor's visits may eventually become free. Giving people basic coverage and treatment for ailments, but when it comes to exotic, complex medicines and procedures, it will still cost patients some money. Also, research and development in these areas creating new products will also be profitable. I feel there is an opening in this vicinity.

I also feel that free healthcare will take years to become law. Having insurance will continue to be the norm. Paying for procedures, medical devices, and medicine, will drive the healthcare industry.

Some of the healthcare stocks I favor are Johnson & Johnson (JNJ), Pfizer (PFE), Merck (MRK), Abbott Laboratories (ABT), Bristol-Myers Squibb (BMY), and Eli Lilly (LLY). These companies are US companies with international exposure. They are all profitable and pay great dividends.

Financials

One of the most dangerous sectors of late, which regularly every twenty to thirty years implodes, is the financial sectors. The last time being the 2007 to 2008 crash of the stock market and especially the financial sector because of bad mortgage deals done by banks and lack of government regulation and oversight, some say caused this crash. People, for the most part, were buying more houses than they could afford. And banks were allowing this and were investing in or wagering that people would default on these massive mortgages. Many banks and financial institutions were bankrupt or had lost billions. Also, Bank of America and Citigroup will be profitable again, but as an investor, are you willing to wait several years for this turnaround to occur? They currently pay a very small dividend. I recommend Wells Fargo and JP Morgan.

Telecommunication Services

This sector is the telephone and cell phone, bandwidth, fixed-line, wireless, fiber-optic networks, cellular, and other communication. This sector primarily has companies like AT&T and Verizon Communications as its pillars. This sector consists of a few slow-growing stocks that pay high dividends. I like Verizon Communication (VZ) because they are buying up spectrum quickly so they can expand their networks and 4G.

Materials

This sector includes metals, minerals, chemical, glass, and paper companies. Materials sector is made up of DuPont (DD), Monsanto (MON), and Dow Chemical (DOW), within this sector mining stocks like Freeport-McMoRan Copper & Gold (FCX) and Newmont Mining (NEM).

Industrials

The industrial sector has one of the oldest survivors of the Dow. This sector is made up of aerospace and defense, transportation, infrastructure, construction, and buildings. General Electric (GE), United Technologies (UTX), Caterpillar (CAT), Union Pacific (UNP), and Boeing (BA) are a few powerhouse stocks from this sector.

Energy

The energy sector, or Big Oil, is the next sector we will talk about. This sector consists of some of the heavyweight in the world. Companies like ExxonMobil (XOM), Chevron (CVX), Schlumberger (SLB), and Haliburton (HAL) make up top stocks in this sector. This sector does exploration, production, refining of oil, and gas products.

Technology

This sector also called information technology, or IT for short, which includes technology, software, and services. I endorse stocks like Microsoft (MSFT), Intel (INTC), Apple (APPL), International Business Machine (IBM), and Google (GOOG), from this sector.

Introduction

You should hold on to stocks that you have in your portfolio. Don't sell unless you have some type of emergency in your life. As Jeremy Siegal has said, "You should be investing in stocks for the long run." His books are classics and should be read by everyone, including eager, young investors. It's important to buy stocks for the long term and invest in dividend-paying stocks. When a stock market crash occurs, many people panic as on May 6, 2010. The Dow Jones dropped over 1,000 points during midday trading, losing 700 points in 15 minutes. It was chaos. There was rioting in the streets of Athens, Greece.

S&P was down 1 percent on the day. Gold was over 1,200 dollars, up 30 points. It seems like the world was coming to an end. The Dow ended that day down 3.20 percent or 347.80, closing at 10,520.32. So if you would have sold midday, you would have lost huge. For example, Proctor & Gamble, a stock which I own, was down 20 points midday to around 40 dollars, a blue-chip stock. If you would have sold at noon, say 100 shares at 42 with an opening price 61.91, it would have been a tremendous loss. It ended the day around 60. This is an example of why you should hold on to stocks. If you panicked, it would have cost you almost 2,000 dollars. In one day, the stock swung 20 points.

Large Cap Stocks with Dividends

These stocks are some of the best household names out there. They can be called blue chips, which are the best large-cap stocks out there. McDonald's (MCD) and Wal-Mart (WMT) are examples of two. These huge companies are everywhere all across the great country of the USA and around the world.

When configuring any portfolio, dividends are crucial for you to receive higher returns on your money. Dividends should be fully reinvested into the company's stock. Therefore, if you buy stock every month and are being paid a quarterly dividend and are reinvesting dividends, you can see how easy it is to accumulate shares quickly.

Most dividends are paid quarterly, or every four months. Some are also paid once a year, and a few companies pay them monthly; that's right, once a month.

Strategy No. 10: Buy and Hold!

This strategy consists of an investor buying a stock, usually that pays a dividend, and never selling it no matter how bad or good it performs. Buy and hold! Some say you should do this with a large cap dividend stock, which we discussed earlier. Some say buy and hold for the longest possible timeframe, forever. Some say buy and homework. I say it's a combination of all three. I believe in doing your research before you put your hard-earned money into the stock market. Understanding your company's earnings, cash flow, debt, and other important statistics that will help you determine that you have a good stock now and in the future, with continued analysis of these stocks. And once you have found that stock, keep it for a long, long time.

Pepsi (PEP)

Pepsi manages beverage and snack food businesses worldwide. The company also sells healthier, grain-based foods along with its snacks and soda business that includes brands like Pepsi, Mountain Dew, Tropicana, and Quaker Oats. They also have the most popular sports drink, Gatorade. Market cap is around 103 billion.

McDonald's (MCD)

McDonald's controls fast-food restaurants around the world. These restaurants are the home of the Big Mac, Chicken McNugget, Filet O'Fish, and the best fries in the world. Market cap is about 100 billion.

Verizon (VZ)

Verizon is a telecommunications company that provides wired line voice, cable television, data, wireless, and internet services. They also provide network services for the federal government. Its wireless division recently added Apple's iPhone. Market cap is 105 billion.

Walt Disney (DIS)

The Walt Disney Company is an entertainment company that works in media networks, motion picture entertainment, theme parks and resorts, cruise lines, consumer products, and interactive media. Walt Disney has media channels like ESPN and ABC, along with a hoard of past and present Disney children's motion pictures in their archive. Market cap is 74 billion.

Dominion Resources (D)

Dominion Resources is a cluster of diversified utility holding companies that generates, transmits, distributes, and sells electric energy in Virginia and North Carolina. Market cap is about 28 billion.

Pfizer (PFE)

Pfizer is a research-based, global biopharmaceutical corporation that discovers, develops, manufactures, and markets medicines for humans and animals. This company is a giant in this industry. Pfizer, the parent company, and a spin-off is possible. Market cap of the company is about 165 billion.

General Electric (GE)

General Electric is a conglomerate industrial that produces products ranging from aircraft engines, water treatment, power generation, household appliances, and consumer finances. Market cap is around 209 billion.

ExxonMobil (XOM)

ExxonMobil is a large global energy business involving the exploration for and production of crude oil, natural gas, and petroleum products. Market cap is around 404 billion.

DuPont (DD)

DuPont is a worldwide chemical company involved in manufacturing, seed production, producing of chemicals, agriculture, and plastics. Market cap is around 50 billion.

MasterCard (MA)

MasterCard is a worldwide payment solutions organization that provides a variety of services in support of credit and debit card programs for financial institution. It offers transaction processing services for credit and debit cards, electronic cash, and automated machines. Market cap is about 52 billion.

If you like Coca-Cola (KO) instead of Pepsi (PEP) . . .
If you like Visa (V) instead of MasterCard (MA) . . .

These blue-chip stocks are my suggestions to you. By all means, my picks are not the end all know all. I want to open your eyes to what stocks will give you your foundation. Build your foundation, and then you can take a few chances on more volatile stocks. But, by all means, a core of 5 to 10 stocks to begin with.

Chapter 4

International Stocks

Today, because we are living in a global environment, international stocks are pivotal to your portfolio. Jeremy J. Siegal states in *Stocks for the Long Run*, "Any analysis of the stock market today must be international in scope." He says this to show how important the role of international business plays in an American economy. So, as an investor, you want to take advantage of this knowledge and incorporate this into your asset account.

I have lived overseas, and that has helped me bring to light how much all these very different countries are so reliant on each other. This is a global economy; therefore, investing in international stocks is pivotal. My uncle told me when I was young that we live in a global economy and that you should think accordingly.

Buying Chinese stock is dangerous mainly because of accounting flaws, irregularities, and outright deception of their financial balance sheet. I recommend no Chinese stocks, I believe, because of their bad balance sheets and hot stocks, which are just bad rip-offs of American companies. These companies should not be owned in your portfolio of stocks. There are many other international companies that you can invest in. China is not a place where I want you or your money.

Now, I can give you some positives about China and how you can play China without the exposure to Chinese stock. China has the fastest growing middle class in the world. That means they want what American middle class families have—a Chevy or Ford (F) in the driveway, an iPhone, and whatever else is extremely popular in America at the time. The way to make money of this growing demographic is to invest in American companies that have coverage to China. Apple (AAPL) is an excellent example of a company with this publicity. Be careful of slowdowns in China; this may affect your China-exposed stock.

Investing in the UK is just like buying in America. Putting your money in the UK is good for your portfolio. It is as good as American securities. The UK has companies like Diageo (DEO) and British Petroleum (BP). These stocks can give you the diversification that you need in your portfolio.

Strategy No. 11: International Flavor

In this section, I will talk to you about international stocks that I like and should go in your portfolio. This gives your portfolio international flavor. It is important that international stocks be in your core portfolio; whether we like it or not, we are a global economy. We are intertwined country to country. There is an old saying, "America sneezes, the rest of the world catches a cold."

Some of the stocks to own or that I recommend buying are international stocks, which I will give a brief description of below:

Sanofi (SNY)

Sanofi (SNY) is a French-based worldwide pharmaceutical company yielding almost 5 percent. The healthcare company manages complex diseases such as diabetes solutions, human vaccines, innovative drugs, consumer healthcare, and animal healthcare.

Roche (RHHBY)

Roche (RHHBY) is a Swiss pharmaceutical and diagnostics company. Roche is the world leader in, in vitro diagnostics and drugs for cancer, transplantation, and in other therapeutic areas with a high medical need.

Diageo (DEO)

Diageo (DEO) is a United Kingdom-based company selling beers and spirits.

Novo Nordisk (NVO)

Novo Nordisk (NVO) is a Denmark global healthcare company specializing in making insulin and has over thirty thousand employees in numerous countries. They have two divisions for diabetes and biopharmaceutical. Their diabetes division has modern insulin products, and their biopharmaceutical has growth hormone and hormone replacement therapy.

Teva Pharmaceuticals (TEVA)

Teva Pharmaceuticals (TEVA) is an Israeli international generic base pharmaceutical that develops and produces with over forty-five thousand employees globally.

Sasol (SSL)

Sasol (SSL) is a South African-integrated energy and chemical company. This company produces natural gas and oil, mines coal, and refines imported crude oil in Africa.

HDFC Bank (HDB)

HDFC Bank (HDB) is an Indian-based bank industry. The company has interest earnings, retail banking, transaction banking, and wholesale banking. The institution has over two thousand nationwide network.

Vina Concha y Toro (VCO)

Vina Concha y Toro (VCO) is a Chile-based wine company. It also is a producer, bottler, and exporter. The corporation has a winery and vineyards in Argentina.

Toyota Motors (TM)

Toyota Motors (TM) is a Japanese automobile and financial business. The company designs, builds, sells cars, and parts and accessories. The Toyota Camry is one of its top-selling automobiles.

Turkcell (TKC)

Turkcell (TKC) is a Turkey-based telecommunication corporation. The company has mobile services such as mobile voice and internet over its GSM-based mobile communication network.

Veolia Environment (VE)

Veolia Environment (VE) is a French water, environment, and infrastructure business. The institution has major businesses in water management, waste treatment and recovery, energy efficiency and mobility.

Diana Shipping (DSX)

Diana Shipping (DSX) is a Greek worldwide provider of shipping and transportation services. The industry has twenty-six dry bulk carriers that transport cargoes.

Royal Dutch Shell (RDS)

Royal Dutch Shell (RDS) is a Dutch global group of energy and petrochemical businesses. Some of its companies are oil and gas industry, crude oil and natural gas, and transportation of gas.

Posco (PKX)

Posco (PKX) is a South Korean-incorporated steel-producing company. This company has a variety of steel products that are used for vessels, consumer electronics, vehicles, and robotic and building structures.

British Petroleum (BP)

British Petroleum (BP) is a United Kingdom-based oil corporation. The corporation provides fuel for transportation, petrochemical products, retail services, and energy.

Rio Tinto (RTP)

Rio Tinto (RTP) is a United Kingdom metals and mining business. The company has underground mills, mines, and refineries where they produce gold, copper, diamonds, aluminum, and iron ore.

Corpbanca SA (BCA)

Corpbanca SA (BCA) is Chile's largest bank. This institution includes over one hundred branches in Chile with commercial and retail banking services.

Total (TOT)

Total (TOT) is a French oil company. This business employs over 90,000 people worldwide in 130 countries. It has industry segments of oil and natural gas exploration, liquefied natural gas, crude oil and petroleum products.

Siemens (SI)

Siemens (SI) is a German electrical engineering conglomerate, which has products in the energy, healthcare, industry, and infrastructure sectors.

Here are a few international selections from my portfolio vault. They are a few companies from all over the world. These companies range from banks to oil to telecommunication companies. As always, do your research on these companies, which may pay a dividend, and to understand the tax rules for some of these international stocks.

International stocks give your portfolio an extra layer of diversification. When blue chips in the United States are performing badly, look to these stocks to boost your returns. Keep in mind that most of the stocks I will recommend pay a dividend of some sort. So during international downturns with a dividend, you will get paid to wait for that upward swing or recovery in the foreign market.

Free Trade—foreign countries purchasing US goods and the United States purchasing foreign countries' goods. US corporations rely on their products being placed on foreign shelves and vice versa. This will increase profits for both sides, as well as familiarity, and product loyalty. US businesses regularly place their products in growing and booming populations, as well as underdeveloped countries to help profitable margins.

The risk of investing overseas can be tremendous at times. Foreign countries like all countries have leadership, economic social uprising, military standoffs, political battles, and currency problems that may, at times, rear its ugly head in a country. Please understand that these are only some of the issues you will have to keep an eye on if you invest in the stock in international countries.

In foreign countries, regulations are usually more lenient and relaxed. Taxes are more often lower than in America, giving companies more incentives to do business in distant countries.

Anytime, Anywhere . . .

You can trade stock anywhere in almost any market around the world at anytime if you're living overseas around the world as many of our men and women in uniforms are doing.

With the dawn of the internet, more than ever, we are a global economy. We are connected in so many different ways. You can trade or buy and sell stock anywhere with a computer and internet access and the ability to get to your brokerage sites.

Do not think because you are living in a distant land that you will not be able to invest. Technology has afforded us a way to communicate and manage your money online whenever you want. Manage your money in any time zone across any land.

Chapter 5

New School vs. Old School

Strategy No. 12: Old School vs. New School

Introduction

In investing, there are two very different approaches of investing. They are what my father and grandfather invested in and what I invested in, in my earlier twenties years. I call this new-school vs. old-school portfolios. Your age may be the most influential factor in how you build your portfolio. Depending on your age dictates the formulation of the stocks you own. Whether you are twenty-three or one hundred, wherever you are in your journey, will display your portfolio design. Younger generations will think differently from older ones. This is because different ages reveal various goals and accumulated wealth levels.

Old School

A fifty-two-year-old, three years from retirement. He's looking for consistency, the same old stuff, doesn't want anything to rock his boat or his portfolio. He has his portfolio set up so that every month he gets a dividend payment that is reinvested from his various stocks. That's right, twelve months of a dividend payment each month. Three more years and he'll get a monthly check from that portfolio. Most of his stocks are yielding 3 percent or more, no need to check his portfolio; he knows that it's doing the same thing it was doing twenty years ago, pumping out cash.

First, let's start out with old-school portfolios; these are very conservative stocks—phone companies, the Ma Bells, the telephone companies or your local gas and electric company, or railroads. I guarantee you that if you look at anybody's portfolio who is over forty-five years of age that is invested in stocks nine times out of ten you will find that it is filled with conservative stocks of their time. General Electric (GE) and Proctor & Gamble (PG) are probably in those accounts as well. Old-school investors use Yahoo and Barron's for their research. *Nightly Business Report* is a television show that old-school investors watch. This is a straightforward, no-nonsense show that gives you facts about what took place in the financial market. Utilities are also a huge staple in an old-school portfolio.

When constructing an old-school portfolio, the first question you ask is, Does this stock pay a dividend and is it sustainable?

Patience is what you must have with an old-school portfolio. Time is an asset. Dividends compounding year after year along with moderate appreciation of the stock is what you covet.

Value stocks that have strong company fundamentals are what should be purchased. These blue chips, highly recognized companies have shown fundamental growth of 5-7 percent at least and that combined with not only dividends but year after year dividend growth.

Your old-school portfolio consists of conservative stock choices, those stocks that can be called the trusted and true. The Pfizer (PFE), General Electric (GE), Proctor & Gamble (PG) stocks that have been around for a hundred years, your father's or even grandfather's portfolio. These dividend payers are not fancy. They will not give you huge stock price swings up or down. Also, because of the 3 percent and above dividend, you will be able to sleep at night.

Think in terms of products that use in your house. I was taught when you begin to construct a portfolio *buy what you own!* This means buy the stocks of products that you use in your house. Buy what you own! General Electric (GE) household appliances, Microsoft (MSFT) software on your computer, Clorox(CLX) bleach under your sink, Proctor & Gamble (PG) Tide detergent to wash your clothes. Please buy what you own! These are the products that you use day in and day out.

Old-school portfolios put you in a defensive state of mind. You are willing to take 5-10 percent gains in addition to dividends year after year. You shun volatility and quick trading. You have kept the same old-school portfolio for years with minor changes. You look for out-of-favor companies that were blue chips. The company could have had a couple of bad earning quarters and are ripe for the picking.

Old-school portfolios are conservative common stocks that consist of high-yielding dividends. These dividends usually range from 3.5-7 percent. For this portfolio, growth is not a concern. It is yield and annual income that is paramount to the investor. Utilities make up a huge portion of the old-school portfolio. Duke Energy (DUK), Dominion Resources (D), Southern (SO), Exelon (EXC), Con Edison (ED), to name a few; they have been in these income investors' portfolios for years. At this time, these stocks yield 3.5 percent to nearly 6 percent. Giving you the income you need especially if you are a retiree or are in need of income. Transportation is another sector specifically railroads such as CSX (CSX), Union Pacific (UNP), Norfolk Southern (NSC), which should be highlighted. Railroads have been a part of transporting goods across the United States for over 100 years. These dividend payers consistently pay dividends year after year.

Another sector that passes the old-school test is seasoned stocks in health care like Pfizer (PFE), Johnson & Johnson (JNJ), Merck (MRK), and Abbott Labs (ABT).

Old School: Time and Age

The longer you hold your dividend-paying stocks and the more time you are in your positions, the more shares and appreciation you get from your stocks. Your old-school portfolio is full of this type of dividend-paying stock. These are the stocks that you have held longer than your oldest child's age. You have made time work for you and your portfolio. Your portfolio produces so much passive income that your comfortable retirement is just around the corner.

If you're an older adult, this suggests that you can put away as much money as you can in a conservative portfolio if you are preretirement.

New School

Imagine a twenty-three-year-old fresh out of school, risk and chance on their mind. She's got her iPod on one hip and her cell, also known as an iPhone, on the other one. Market updates while in her corporate meeting on the job. She is checking her portfolio on her iPhone so they can't be traced on the desktop at work. She thinks, "I can't wait for the Facebook (FB) IPO. I'm going all in." Retirement is some meaningless word that reminds her of her great-uncle and his walking cane, some distant event thirty to forty years away. "What's Apple doing today?" she thinks.

New-school portfolios are what young twenty- to thirty-five-year-olds, who are invested in the latest and greatest fad or technology gizmo such as Apple (AAPL), Google (GOOG), or Facebook (FB), or maybe you're a fan of all three. Most young people buy stocks that do not include dividends. They are riding the wave of investing up and down without getting paid for your suffering. Some of these stocks run up and down. So timing the market is a complicated thing to do. I'm not saying impossible, but it can be difficult to do. With high-flying stocks, it is harder to gauge when to get out especially because of volatility, which means the stock's movement in either direction. These stocks are attractive to young people. They are looking for quick profits or a fast buck. To all my young people just starting out in the investment world, establishing lasting wealth takes some time. New-school investors use Google's financial web page or *Investor's Business Daily* (IBD—newspaper name) to do their research.

New-school portfolios consist of volatile small-growth companies that can make you a lot of money fast, doubling or tripling your money fast. Oh, but there are two sides to every fair coin. You can drop just as fast. These stocks do not usually pay a dividend. They probably come from the technology sector, and their betas are usually well over 1. This means that a stock is riskier because it is higher than the baseline one. They can sometimes be a stock that is part of a new trend or clothing fad.

When buying a growth stock, you forgo dividends for growth. While the company is growing fast, it does not usually pay a dividend. The company is most often in the leading science and technology business. And it feels that instead of paying a dividend, that money can be better spent in research and development.

Risk takers love new-school portfolios; they are looking for growth companies with high double-digit earnings growth year over year.

New-school portfolios tend to change all the time. People that own these stocks tend to be traders. You are probably moving in and out of stocks daily, weekly, or monthly. They rarely are long and hold a stock for years.

New School: Time and Age

At this age, time is your greatest asset along with your collection of stocks. You may have at least forty years before you retire. I know you have seen the charts of money invested in your twenties versus money invested in your forties or fifties and with the goal of retirement at the age of sixty.

Age, along with time, are your two biggest assets. You can make aggressive stock picks and choices, and if they are all bad, be at an age where you can still recover and have a good chunk of wealth in your portfolio. In your twenties and early thirties, take some risk. Your portfolio will thank you later in your sixties.

Conclusion

Bringing everything together with old-school versus new-school portfolios, combining the old and new thought can bring together a powerful portfolio. Listening to older citizens and talking with them about their collection of stocks beyond mutual funds can be rewarding. So they can teach you some of the history of investing. To the young people, listening is important. To my older generation, take time with young people. They need your old-school train of thought including your cliques and humorous advice.

By taking these two strategies and applying them to your portfolio, you get the best of both worlds. You get risk and conservatism together. You get to sleep at night and take a long shot. By applying both these investment concept to your group of stocks, you get a balance between the two. By getting large potential stock growth, along with compounding dividends, you get what I call an ideal portfolio. Ideal, in the fact, that this is what every investor wants in a portfolio—both sides of the spectrum all in one. You are playing on both sides of the fences. So bring these strategies together and watch your portfolio blossom. If you try, it will definitely be worth it.

Do not think you have to be either old school or new school. You do not have to be one or the other. Most people start out new school when they are young 20-32 and become old school 48-99. The area where I am trying to get you to concentrate on is the ages 33-47 when most have a combination of both styles of investing in their portfolio.

Chapter 6

Speculation

Most people think that speculation is a new topic in investing, but I'm here to tell you it is not. Investors have been discussing, in text, investor speculation as early as the mid to late 1800s. That's right, dating back to the 1850s, as stated by most researchers. Some of the greatest investors of all time have conversed on this topic through their writings.

In a 2010 *Barron's* article, they conversed about an index that had a few stocks that were consumer stocks or stocks that are trendy. Those stocks listed were Bed Bath & Beyond (BBBY), Nike (NKE), Urban Outfitters (URBN), automotives, and some airline stocks. I feel you should stay away from these types of stocks because styles and taste change all the time. People like one thing one day and another thing, another. Automotives are another stock that needs to be heavily analyzed by you, the investor. Trends in cars come and go for a while. People, for the most part, bought American cars especially from the 1940s to 1980s. During the 1990s-2000s, a lot of foreign cars were purchased, Japanese cars, with Toyota (TM) and Honda (HMC) leading the way. General Motors (GM) collapsed, and Toyota (TM) had major recalls, so Honda (HMC) was now leading the way. Finally, General Motors (GM) made its most recent comeback, driven through sales in China and United States Auto Bailout.

Small Speculative or Unseasoned Companies

Speculation can mean companies that are not stable in the traditional form.

Some companies are small and not making a lot of money. They may have small market cap in the tens to hundreds of millions. They may not be very profitable yet and may have only a few employees. They may be just starting out, or they may be going through a rough couple of quarters and have been abandoned by shareholders. These are companies that are unheard of and overlooked. These are the companies that you hear whispers about. These are the companies that are talked about in the back smoke rooms between distinguished gentlemen in tailored suits.
It is okay to speculate on one or two stocks. It is okay to add some risk to your group of stocks, but the majority of your portfolio shouldn't be speculative.

Many authors define speculation as gambling, pure and simple. Speculation, I believe, has very many layers and that the previous definition tells only part of the story. It is one of the most confusing topics in investing and can be described in many different forms. Speculation has been deemed as a negative way to play the market.

Be wary of speculation on commodities like oil, equities, bonds, and currencies where speculators take enormous risk on predicting future volatile movements up and down in order to gain profits.

Chapter 7

Don't Invest Your Rent
or Mortgage Money

When you have put aside a small emergency fund and have started working fresh out of school. Once you have these things done, that is the opportune time to start investing. You do not want to invest your rent or mortgage money. You must invest free money that you have after paying all your bills.

Start off slow; some stocks will even let you get in at twenty-five dollars a month. This is even lower than the fifty dollars a month I discussed earlier. You can always raise the amount that you contribute or lower it. So take your time and contribute slowly and confidently.

How do I come up with twenty-five or fifty dollars a month? Easy, miss a few parties or social gatherings a month. There is always another party. I figured this out in school. My friends used to say, "Man, you missed the greatest party ever, the best party of the century." And that was always until the next weekend when the greatest party of all time happened again. My response is it's always another party. I'll catch the next one. So miss a few parties and take that money and put it toward your future. Instead of partying every weekend, try twice a month, and if you party twice a month, try once a month. Meet up with friends for brunch once a month instead of twice a month. Talk to them on the phone, send them an e-mail, text them to stay in touch, or use Facebook (FB). You can use the extra money to fund your retirement.

Not much of a partier? Here are a small number of other ways to come up with the twenty-five to fifty dollars a month. Whatever habits you have, good or bad, cut back on them or eliminate it if you can. This includes coffee, that is, expensive lattes, and so on. Buy instant coffee from the grocery store preferably in bulk. I drink my coffee in the morning black, and yes, it is an acquired taste that takes some getting used to. No sugar, no cream, and best of all, no expensive lattes for me. Now back to topic, subscriptions, whether it's premium cable or unread magazines and newspapers, are a few things that should be on the chopping block. Also, any luxurious and unneeded shopping sprees can be thrown into this category as well. So no matter what you do, be creative with it!

Strategy No. 13: Automatic Investing

Fifty dollars a month can and will get you in the game. What game? The investment game of course. Automatically, investing fifty dollars a month can slowly get you to financial freedom. Keep in mind that I am not offering instant gratification or overnight riches. This is a slow accumulation of wealth, a gradual ascend.

By investing automatically, it takes the guesswork out of what to do with my money this month. You do not have to remember to write checks each month. You can set it and forget it. You can usually set it for the first, fifteenth, and/or the thirtieth, which will then be withdrawn from your checking or savings account on those days each month. This is very easy to do, just follow instructions on your computer.

Fifty dollars is just the beginning, as you can get pay raises and cost-of-living raises on your job. You can up your contributions to a hundred, two hundred fifty, three hundred fifty, five hundred dollars, or whatever new dollar amount you can now afford.

Automatic investing is one of your most powerful investment tools along with compounding. One simple effort can lead to a lifetime of wealth. That's what millionaires do; small efforts lead to big rewards.

Chapter 8

Dogs of the Dow

Strategy No. 14: Dogs of the Dow

This is a strategy that is put in place for investing. This strategy has to do with every year buying the worst performing stock in the Dow Jones Industrial Average every year that is paying the highest yield. I tend to buy the top three stocks that are in the Dow component with the highest yield and, in theory, change every year. In a second, I will give you a more detailed outline of the dogs of the Dow theory.

Michael B. O'Higgins made the dogs of the Dow strategy famous around 1991. Basically by saying if blue-chip dividend-paying stocks have a low price and high dividend, that company is worth more and will eventually rise in stock price because the fundamentals of the company are there. The stock price will rise, and the company will go from a high-yielding, low-price stock to a low-yielding, high-price stock in theory.

Dogs of the Dow strategy is to basically, at the beginning of the year on January 1, 2013, pick the highest yielding stocks in the Dow, usually the top ten yielders, and hold them for an entire year. The year after on January 1, 2014, the next year, hold the stocks that are in the highest yielding top ten and replace the ones that have been successful and risen out of the ten yielders.

If you combine this strategy with dollar-cost averaging (DCA), you can have a strong, powerful plan of action for investing. DCA by itself has been criticized as not being an effective plan saying that if the price goes up continuously, you will be buying at steadily higher prices, which I think is a flawed argument. The majority of individual investors do not have large sums of money to invest like five thousand, ten thousand, and twenty thousand to invest at a time; so DCA is an outstanding way to build your shares in a proven company for the little investor. The numbers and arithmetic of DCA may not work as an investment strategy, but for the small investor, it's the way to get in. I am an advocate for the little guy or the small-time investor battling his way to wealth.

Combining dogs of the Dow and dollar-cost averaging, you are buying the lowest costing highest yielding stock in small amounts overtime. So while you are waiting for the share value to improve, you are getting dividends. These dividends should be reinvested. And you are purchasing more and more shares at the lower rate, and as share price rises, you buy fewer shares at the higher price.

When picking from the Dow Thirty stocks, it is good to pick a stock that is riding high and one that is hanging low. In other words, pick a few stocks that are performing well, one or two stocks that have risen greatly and pick two or three that are dogs and have performed poorly. This will do two things: first to ensure you are diverse, which is always important in many different sectors, and second, give you some winners to go along with your high yielders.

Choosing among Dow stocks in the same sector can be tricky. If you have two stocks that are in the Dow that have been dogs in the same sector, choose the one with the smaller market cap. For instance, AT&T (T) and Verizon (VZ) are both dogs yielding over 5 percent. You should choose Verizon, the smaller market cap stock, which has more room to grow.

It is also okay if you own two stocks in the same sector. Grab a stock or choose the best one, it's up to you and how you manage your portfolio. You are in control. But diversity is our prime objective, keep that in mind at all times.

Staying diverse within the Dow can be tough. Normally within sectors, the stocks move together; when stocks are doing badly with high yields, they are usually in the same sector again. Verizon (VZ) and AT&T (T), or Pfizer (PFE) and Merck (MRK) are some examples of this.

When investing, the Dow is the best place to start. As I stated earlier, the Dow should make up the core of your portfolio. The Dow is diverse and has mostly profitable and stable companies. Look to the Dow to start building a portfolio of stocks.

This is a strategy that has come under a ton of scrutiny mainly because you are getting rid of winners and buying stocks that have underperformed. Use caution when you're supposed to dump those winners at the beginning of the year.

Chapter 9

Stocks Under $12

During the financial crisis, financial stocks took a huge dive, two stocks Bank of America (BAC) and Citigroup (C). I purchased both stocks based on some research, and a family member told me that this has happened before and similar crises have happen in the financial industry during the late 1970s with the savings and loan crisis. These stocks, for the most part, have underperformed with Bank of America stuck under ten dollars a share and Citigroup doing a reverse split of ten for one, that is, for every ten shares they take from you, you get one share, and the price jumps up ten times its original price. Wow! Over the last five years, these financial businesses have been stagnant, pretty scary for an investor.

It normally does not pay to play in this realm! I mean, investing in low-valued stocks, fewer than twelve dollars, is not a very good investing strategy. Stocks that have been beaten down to this valuation are not worth purchasing, unless they began to show signs that their fundamentals are improving and that they are profitable. Also, if they have cut their dividend in the past and now have begun to increase them over a few years. Momentum investors beware because the pendulum can and will swing in both ways. These stocks can go up above twelve dollars or down to two or three dollars a share. There are always exceptions to the rule I have given you; just always be cautious and get a dividend.

I'm not talking to my friends that are dealing in options. When twelve dollar and under stocks can be worth wild and ideal when writing covered calls in option trading. For the most part, we are keeping things simple. So that is another book for another time.

Back to the subject at hand, cheap stocks can be trouble. You are taught that cheaper is better. That the cheaper you can get a product or service, the better. The term *discounted* is thrown around and, at a lesser rate, discussed.

What is missing? The term is quality! When you purchase quality goods at a discounted rate that is goal, that is a deal! When you go to Whole Foods (WFM) or Safeway (SWY), you are looking for quality food, but what if there is a sale or several discounted items in the store? You got a high-quality product for cheaper than the retail price.

People are constantly buying cheap, bad products that are not good, fall apart, or that are not good for you. These scenarios are exactly what people do when they come across cheap stocks. They do not do the research and see if this stock is a quality stock. Yes, it is discounted, but is it quality? Is this fish fresh, or is it decaying and rotten? Which do you want on your dinner table tonight? Quality stocks are your ally in your portfolio.

So how do you figure out which discounted stocks are healthy enough to put in your portfolio? Well, ask a couple of questions: (1) Is the company making money, or are their earnings positive? (2) Does the stock pay a dividend? (3) Is the dividend sustainable? Its earnings need to be more than three times the quarterly dividend. (4) And the stock has to be over five dollars. Do not buy any stock fewer than five dollars. The reward is not worth the risk. Protect your money and portfolio.

Chapter 10

Manage Your Own Money

In light of the 2008 finance crisis, it is in my opinion that most people should manage their own money through the stock market. There is an old saying, "pick your own poison," which lightheartedly means win, lose, or draw with a portfolio of your own stocks that you pick and do research with. Relying on a broker can cost an enormous amount in fees and service charges over time.

We have talked a lot about different financial terms. We discussed portfolios, capitalization size, dividends, and other concepts. With as little as fifty dollars per month, I will show you how to create, manage, control your portfolio, and put yourself on the road to wealth.

First, we will have to make a decision on where to put the fifty dollars or more that you are saving each month. The first choice is to directly buy the stock through a dividend reinvestment plan (DRIP). Not all stocks have this plan, but if they do, you can be an owner of stock for as little as twenty, fifty, or a hundred dollars a month depending on the plan. There are a couple of companies that have direct relationships with Fortune 500 companies that you can invest in. The major one that I use is Computershare. They have a website www. computershare.com, where you can sign up for the stock of your choice from their list. If you are not comfortable filling out the paperwork online, you may request it via mail. Some of the stocks that have a DRIP plan are McDonald's (MCD), Johnson

& Johnson (JNJ), ExxonMobil (XOM), and Altria (MO). The dividend of these plans can be reinvested, sometimes for a few dollars charge, and sometimes for free. You can write a check for fifty dollars a month or have it withdrawn from your checking or saving account on the first or fifteenth or both. If you still have trouble figuring out the website, pick a stock from the list provided and contact Computershare directly by phone.

All right that was step 1 in creating a portfolio and a path to wealth. The next step is to get you into a discount brokerage account or full-service brokerage account or both.

I have a full-service brokerage account with an individual account, Rollover IRA, and a Roth IRA. I also have an account in a discount brokerage account. I recommend that you manage your own money. If you set up your own accounts correctly, it is easy to do. I also think it is important to have your money in a large brokerage firm that is FDIC protected up to 250,000 dollars.

Discount brokerage firms are good for small investors. Computershare, Sharebuilder, E*Trade, and Ameritrade are great discount brokerage firms that let you trade stock with extremely low fees. This allows you to buy and sell stock cheaper than the major brokerage firms. You will see free trades, one-dollar trades, and two-dollar trades with discount firms. You do not need to hire someone to manage your money for you. You do not need to pay a financial advisor 1-3 percent commission on your portfolio a year or as much as three hundred dollars an hour to manage your money. Do it yourself and keep your money in your pocket. As long as you're responsible and can do a small amount of research twice a month, go for it. Call your own shots.

Full-brokerage firms are financial institutions, where you can trade, get financial advice and a financial advisor. When your sum of money begins to swell, consider putting your money in a firm like T. Rowe Price, Fidelity, Charles Schwab, or Morgan Stanley. Trading here in these firms can cost you $21.99, $18.99, $9.99, or $6.99, depending on the value of your account.

A financial planner has a major duty to protect your portfolio against high risk, loss, and inflation. Why, they are supposed to not only do that but increase your portfolio's value and give you the high, single-digit and low, double-digit returns that most people would like.

Do these financial planners have your best interest in mind, or are they recommending the financial instruments that will make them the most money and not you?

I want you to make the decision. Who has my best interest in mind? I will never allow someone else to manage my money because it is something that you can do on your own, and with a little study and reading, you can become quite good at it. And I do not mean a lot of education or schooling. But by reading some financial literature from time to time, you can greatly improve your financial IQ, that's all.

I am not saying that you should never ever talk to a financial planner. By all means, let them give you a free overview of your financial situation. More than likely, they are going to tell you: (1) You need to get out of debt, and of course, they have a plan for that; (2) You need at least three to six months of your living expenses saved up; (3) You are probably behind on saving for your retirement, but and I do mean but, I (financial planner) can help you put together a plan to help with all these situations and help you reach your retirement goals, and all

I get is commission or the new one is fee-based advisors for our high-end investor! Use their guidance to put together your own financial plan for free. Roll up your sleeves and get started immediately. The sooner the better get to it.

Chapter 11

Initial Public Offerings (IPOs)

Strategy No. 14: Initial Public Offering

IPOs are initial public offerings. IPOs are the first public sale of stock by a private company to the general public. Why would a company go public? Most companies go public to have access to cheaper capital and more financing options.

Investing in IPOs can be one of the greatest and most powerful actions that you can do to your portfolio. An IPO can add a 20 percent or greater boast to your initial investment, depending on value, how much stock you buy and if you choose the correct stock. Throughout this chapter, I will guide you through this process. What do you look for in an IPO? Which types of IPOs to avoid? How to analyze a company before it goes public and where to find information on these companies?

They can make you a huge amount of money especially if you know how to pick them. You should pick medium to large cap profitable companies. Examples of these are Visa (V), MasterCard (MA), Facebook (FB), and Mead Johnson Nutrition (MJN). These were and are household names, and when companies like these debut, you must buy on a limited order basis. IPOs do not have to be highly risky. Buying quality companies and profitable spin-offs can be very rewarding.

There is usually a window when you purchase IPO shares. I like to wait until after the stock goes public, and during the first two to four months of its issuing is the prime time to buy.

Pricing of an IPO is very important that you observe the range of the stocks. Get a gauge of where the stock will price. What do you think the stock is worth?

When dealing with IPOs, for the most part, stay in the United States. On very hot IPOs, wait a few months before you buy or wait for some type of pull back in the stock. Do not—I repeat—Do not buy the day a company IPOs. This is the biggest mistake people make. By waiting a few weeks or even months, you get a clear look at the company's financial balance sheet. Earnings are very important. So let the IPO companies report one earnings report. If you are unsure about when to purchase, give yourself another month or two to decide if this is the right IPO stock for you.

Some say investing in IPOs is like playing in the lottery or gambling. I feel it is a calculated risk especially if you weed out a few good companies that are profitable. Some people say, "Look at the dot com boom and all the IPOs that eventually went bust." This is very true, and the social media companies going public now look a lot like the dot com boom. And I would not invest in any of them except Facebook (FB). I would do this for a few reasons. First, Facebook (FB) is a leader in social media industry. The company is cutting edge and has only begun to tap its potential. It is the best in its field and barely has any competition. Second, its leadership, Mark Zuckerberg, is one of the most innovative young people in this new sector of social media. Finally, I see Facebook (FB) as the next Google (GOOG). The same hurdles and questions that were being asked about Google (GOOG) are being brought up around economic news channels, blogs, and message boards. Facebook (FB) is the best of the rest and a game changer; do not be shocked if the stock doubles or triples the first day it goes public.

When it comes to IPOs, buy only the best companies and stay away from tech IPOs like software or cloud computing, unless you are confident and have done a ton of research, but do it at your own risk. I will not endorse those companies. When it comes to IPOs, look for leaders in a company or firm. These firms are in a business alone with no competitors, kind of like a monopoly or are far ahead of its competition.

I am going against what most in the finance or economic academia world will tell you not to do. I'm going against the grain on this one.

IPOs should be your last part of the portfolio that you add. Build through buying your blue-chip, large cap, and small cap stocks up positions first in your portfolio.

IPOs give you that blood rush and make you enthusiastic about investing. Your senses heighten and the allure of riches, wealth, and money flash across your mind. One stock, one small investment left alone with all future dividends reinvested could change your life and your portfolio.

During the IPO process, you should be asking yourself a couple of questions about the stock. What product and /or patents does this company have? Is the company profitable? Who is its major competition? These questions will allow you to get a better understanding of your IPO company.

What Types of IPOs to Avoid?

You should avoid IPOs of highly debt-ridden companies for the most part. The small IPOs that is, smaller than two billion, or better known as micro cap, should be avoided over the first few months and watched, studied, and analyzed during this period.

Go to the Securities and Exchange Commission website to view and read the company's S-1 that discusses the company's outlook, past and current earnings.

If you jump into an IPO in the first couple of days, you are competing against traders, who will be jumping in and out of the stock over the first ninety days. They will be looking for quick profits. If this is your goal, I see no problem with taking this position for a short-term investor or trader. For long-term investors, be cautious during this period. And by all means, understand the fact that IPOs are very risky investments. Because of the traders jumping in and out of the stock, the price becomes volatile, with high swings up and down.

Companies that do not have earnings or are not profitable can be dangerous IPO preferences. Be very cautious when purchasing these IPOs. Consider this, do you want to put your hard-earned money in a company who's had no earnings while private and are now going public to get rid of debt and to try and make it profitable.

Before the IPO, when you are thinking of purchasing shares of a company, make sure the company does not own any major debt to a country's government. It is better if they owe money to lenders other than government, preferably private lenders.

Where to Look for Information?

Besides what we have talked about in earlier parts of this chapter, the internet is an excellent source of information, some good and bad. Use of social media via blogs and tweets can be very good sources of information. This opinionated information can be factual or totally made up, so it is up to you to verify these comments.

Chapter 12

Timing and Analyzing the Market

Before we begin to wrap this up, I am going to have to give you a little technical knowledge and analysis. So bear with me as I throw in a couple of baseball analogies in your direction.

P/E Ratio

P/E Ratio means price/earnings ratio. The P/E ratio is the relationship between the current price and expected earnings per share.

Have you ever played baseball or watched America's favorite pastime? Well, if you have, you know a batter has what they call the sweet spot of their bat; this is the place of the thickest part of the bat between the two inches from the top of the bat down to about four inches above the center of the bat. If you hit the ball within that space, the ball is going to jump off the bat and go far, most of the time out of the park. Some of my favorite baseball players do it all the time—Albert Pujols, Josh Hamilton, Derek Jeter, Mickey Mantle, Johnny Bench, and many others. Sometimes you'll see a pitcher in the National League come to bat, and he'll first pitch swing and knock the ball right out the park. A home run by the pitcher of all people, he was doing what no one thought he would.

I want you to be like the pitcher described earlier and pick a good stock that is in the P/E sweet spot, which is between 7 and 15. Find stocks that have that P/E ratio range and good fundamentals and buy them up. That's where you want to swing for the fences. You have your Mickey Mantle and Derek Jeter of the financial investment community who can be compared to Peter Lynch and Warren Buffet who hit a lot of home runs, and you can knock a few out of the park just like them. So knock one out of the park!

Siegel states, "Keep your expectation in line with history. Historically, stocks have returned 6.8 percent after inflation over the last two centuries and have sold at an average P/E ratio of about 15" (360). Here Dr. Siegel is giving us a historical 7 percent return after inflation takes away 2 to 3 percent. This gives you a 10 percent return from stocks over 200 years with an average sweetspot of 15 for its P/E ratio.

Returns of Stocks

Earnings are translated into returns:

> Appreciation in the price of the company's stock is a return of stocks especially if the previous year is compared to the current year and a series of dividend payments made possible by these earnings, throw out the year and added up quarterly to get the year's full and current dividend.

Expected Return = (Current Year Dividend + Capital Appreciation) / (Value of Stock during Period)

Note for **Value of Stocks during Period** take the 52-week range; the low and the high.

So you will have an expected return range!

Chapter 13

Knowing What You Own (Sin Stocks)

Tobacco stocks have been some of the most profitable stocks on record especially Altria (MO). Altria (MO) is currently pays 5.3 percent dividend. Altria (MO), along with other stocks like Lorillard (LO), Reynolds American (RAI), and Philip Morris International (PM), are all powerhouses in the tobacco industry, which is highly profitable, with great balance sheets and tons of cash flow. Altria has a diverse portfolio of companies such as wineries, a partner in SAB Miller (SAB) and its many brands of cigarettes including Marlboro, as well as smokeless and chewing tobacco. People spend anywhere from 6 to 9 dollars a pack for their habit. Imagine if you smoke a pack a day.

Alcohol stocks have been lucrative for years. An example of this is Diageo (DEO), the maker of wine, beer, and spirits. Diageo (DEO) is a British company that has 8 of the top 20 liquors in the world. Captain Morgan and Johnny Walker are a few of these world dominating brands. It also pays a hefty dividend of 3.5 percent. Along with Diageo (DEO), some other alcohol beverages are Anheuser-Busch (BUD). Boston Beer (SAM) is another money-making industry within alcohol.

Gambling and casinos are very profitable stocks, but these stocks are a little more volatile. These casino stocks are international developers of destination properties that attribute premium accommodations and world-class gaming and entertainment. A few of these stocks are Wynn Resorts (WYNN),

Las Vegas Sands (LVS), MGM Mirage (MGM), and Caesars Entertainment (CZR).

Firearms have been a hot stock of late. Sturm, Ruger & Company (RGR) is a small cap company that manufactures and sells firearms. Some of their most popular handheld weapons are especially pistols, rifles, revolvers, and shotguns. Sturm, Ruger (RGR) mainly targets sales of its weapons for the commercial sporting market. These firearms are made in America.

Two Sides to Every Coin: A Moral Dilemma

Heads

When investing, you should know what you own. Investing in things that can harm people is a sticky situation. It is difficult for me to understand in my twenties how much I affected the world around me. I had children, but the only thing I thought about is providing. It seems confusing because it was. During this time, I tried not to take advantage of people because I did not like to be taken advantage of.

Now back to stocks, I invested in Philip Morris in my early twenties; in my thinking, well, I smoked once, so I can invest in it. The stock did and does very well, pays a good dividend, time and again. But as I got into my thirties, I thought, don't I have some sort of obligation to not invest in tobacco that could possibly cause people harm? Why did not I think of this earlier? I believe in God and have Christian beliefs, so my eyes must not have been open to this before.

In my twenties and now ownership is and will always be very important in my life, but make sure you understand what you own and read as much as you can about the history of the companies you own. Educate yourself before you take ownership. History is a funny and enlightening thing, but if you're not careful, it will repeat itself, and that is usually a bad thing. So stay aware.

Tails

It's just a stock, a piece of paper with financial worth! Does this piece of paper affect my spiritual and moral character? Will it make me a better or worse person? I do not worship this bit of paper. It is not my God. All stocks are paper, which can be turned into paper or monetary value, which is just a means of exchange. Don't give it any more power than what it has as a piece of paper. It's just a stock!

There are approximately 70 million smokers worldwide that light up every day. These are adults who do this of their own free will.

No matter what you believe, don't let it affect you and how you invest. Your investment mind set should be different than your ordinary thought process. The investment train of thought is profit driven no more, no less. Winners that grow continuously and pay dividends are what you should be striving for. For the most part, people are good, and to invest in a product that some say is an illegal product such as tobacco would not be sanctioned by most of the world's governments especially not the United States of America. Who am I to say that this product is wrong? It's legal but quite profitable for many countries globally. Investors do just that to invest in companies that will give them a return on their investment. Investing should be driven by your economic views, not your social or political bearings.

Conclusion

The choice is yours; I have laid out two compelling arguments. I am not here to tell you, you are right going with one side or the other. I just want to expose you to this social and sometimes moral dilemma that you may encounter in the investment world when it comes to individual stocks and what you will or will not invest in. Read both sides and see how each makes you feel; this will help you to clarify where you stand on each argument. It's totally up to you; I won't give you any help on this one.

Chapter 14

Giving Back

It is always good to give, from the heart, your money and your time. Donating to the charity of your choice is a great way to start. If you have built a nice retirement portfolio, contribute to your church, youth club, and soup kitchen. You do not have to donate money. I donate clothes I can't wear anymore that are in good condition. Share your wealth with people less fortunate. God has blessed you with health and wealth, so share it with others. You can't take it with you!

Don't have money right now and are still building your wealth? It is also great if you volunteer your time. Spend some time with our youth at the local boys' and girls' club. Mentoring is another way to give back. Working with America's youth is a wonderful way to contribute your knowledge and give them guidance. Our youth need to see positive role models as much as possible so they can learn positive behavior and become future advisers.

Put your charity in your will. So when you pass, your church or organization will receive a portion or your entire investment portfolio. It's up to you. But make sure you give back in any form that you can. We all need each other in this world to participate in everyone's life.

These are all positive acts. By doing these sorts of acts, you are putting others before yourself and enriching your spirituality. Please give often for society's sake. We are all God's children. We take care of each other and treat each other accordingly.

Chapter 15

Reflections

Looking back on my investment career and life, I try to stick to whom and what I know. Consistency is what is important. Know that you're not perfect. Everybody makes mistakes in life and in the investment world. You also put in what you get out. So do your research, and when someone gives you a tip, which they always will, do your research. Investing to me is very therapeutic. I love watching Bloomberg, CNBC, and Fox Business all the time. To me, everything else is entertainment. So make sure that you enjoy life and try to enjoy family as much as you can. I made investing educational as well as entertaining, and you should too. Life gets sometimes difficult, so when it does, make sure you see who is around you and who is talking to you, who calls you. The people giving you a helping hand but not giving you everything. Make sure you keep your head when all about you are losing theirs and blaming it on you. Life keeps changing, and you can't stop it or rewind it. Keep things simple. Life is short, so make sure you show your love to your friends and family.

Once you have taken everything away from someone. What do they have left? Their soul and true ambition is all that remains. This person has nothing else to lose and everything to gain. You have backed them into a corner. There is no way out! Believe in yourself and God and continue on the path onward and upward toward the light.

Investing is fun for me. It is like color to an artist. It is like music notes to a musician.

Take the skills that I have given you, and by all means, give them a try. Invest on your own, experiment with the concepts in this book. Better yet, do not try. Do it! Find your own comfort level with stocks. What are your favorites to own? Figure out what's hot and what's not. Study the fundamentals, earnings, conference calls, management, and the stocks trading range. If you do this analysis, you will be empowered no matter what your stocks you choose.

Good luck on all your future endeavors. Keep God first in your life and don't be afraid to imagine all the opportunities that life has in front of you. Take a chance, and your possibility of succeeding becomes endless. Do not be afraid to do something that you have never done once a month. Do not be afraid of failure. I have failed at many ventures and have had to overcome many obstacles. This is what makes you who you are.

Focus on being constructive and being around optimistic people. This goes beyond investing and stocks and describes how I have coped with life situations and how that has made me a better person and an investor second.

Chapter 16

Conclusion

Financial literacy is an important part of understanding your money. And the stock market is a major portion of this because once you have become a saver, you need to do more with your money than to just save it. You must make your money grow, not just wait for inflation to eat it up. Do not be a saver! Be an investor! Yes, I realize and know the old saying that cash is king. If you want a portion of your money in cash that is fine with me. Another part of financial literacy is making money grow and work even when you can't work anymore. It is my understanding that it is not good to spend more than you are bringing in. Once you have grasped this simple concept, the literacy of finances is all downhill from here.

All these terms, acronyms, and jargon are confusing to me. I'm overwhelmed! That's okay! The stock market and the financial world at large have a lot strange words or verbiage. Keep working on learning a few words at a time and your vocabulary will grow. Do not give up!

Make a plan! When investing, you need to make sure you have a plan of action or whatever you want to call it. I have a systematic set of questions I ask myself before putting together a portfolio. Answer these questions, and you should have very little problems in the way of formulating a portfolio of stocks. This is a method of portfolio building I use and continue to use today. Make your portfolio yours. Own it yourself; combine all my techniques or just a few to make your selection of stocks valuable.

Make a Plan: Guidelines

(1)   What stock do you want to own?
(2)   Are you old school or new school? Dividend or not?
(3)   How much international flavor do you want in your portfolio?
(4)   How many stocks do you want to own?
(5)   Do you want to own speculative stocks?
(6)   Are you diverse?
(7)   Have you picked an IPO stock?
(8)   Will you manage your own money?
(9)   Will you buy into highly profitable so called sin stocks?
(10) How will you give back?

Answering these questions will help you to form a plan of action when amassing your perfect portfolio. Study the company's past performance, look at present earnings, and analyze future or projected earnings. Look at its yield. Understand the products that it sells.

There are a few things that you have to do as an investor in order to be a successful one.

(1)   A portion of your portfolio has to have large cap dividends. These are usually S&P 500 companies. This part of your portfolio is nonnegotiable. You must have some of these companies in your core portfolio. Look to the Dow 30.
(2)   You need some risk. In the form of small cap and IPO stocks. This part of your portfolio is up to you. It's not a necessity, but it is better if you have some

of these stocks in your portfolio. Without some risk, there are no big rewards. Take a shot!

(3) Time. The longer you hold these stocks, especially the large cap, blue-chip dividends payers, the better your portfolio will perform.

Other questions that you can ask yourself. When do I plan to retire? And are you having fun?

Make sure that you are comfortable with whatever stocks you invest in and hold on to in your core portfolio. I want you to understand your investment and to be able to sleep at night.

Oh, and one last thing, did you do your research on that stock before you bought it?

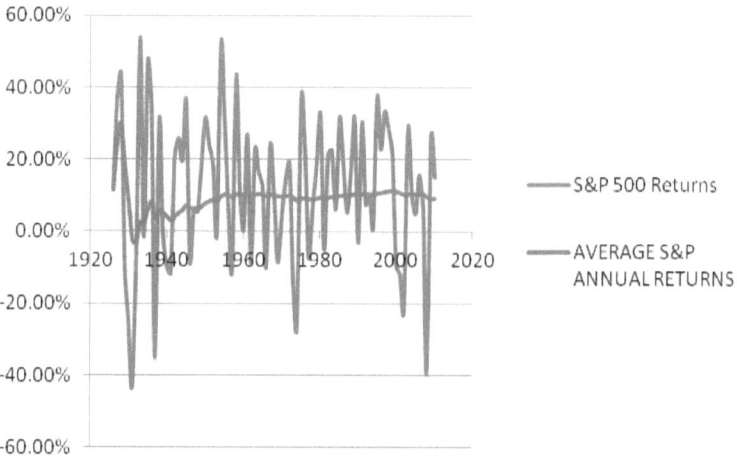

This graph illustrates the year-by-year returns of the S&P 500 along with the average S&P 500 annual returns. At first glance, the S&P 500 returns look unstable, unpredictable and volatile, but the average S&P 500 annual returns have been hovering around 10 percent for the last 50 years. Simply amazing to see!

DOW JONES INDUSTRIAL AVERAGE

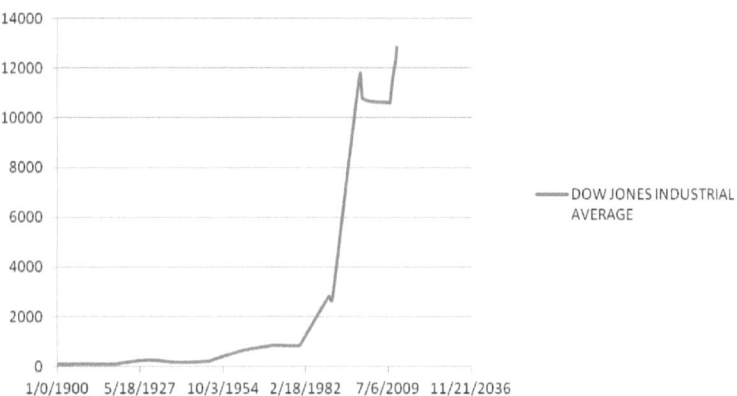

This graph highlights the Dow Jones Industrial Average and shows how, since its inception, it has grown basically exponentially and will continue in this same fashion. When you start investing, look to the Dow 30 to start to amass your stock in your portfolio.

Disclaimer: The views in this book are the authors and you should seek a competent financial advisor before investing.

References

Graham, Benjamin and Jason Zweig. 2003. *The Intelligent Investor: The Definitive Book on Value Investing.* New York: Norton.

Greenblatt, Joel. 1997. *You Can Be A Genius: Uncover The Secret Hiding Places Of Stock Market Profits.* New York: Fireside.

Groppelli, A. A. and Ehsan Nikbakht. 2006. *Barron's Business Review Books Finance.* 5th ed. Barron's Educational Series Inc.

Krass, Peter ed. 1999. *The Book of Investing Wisdom: Writing by Great Stock Pickers and Legends of Wall Street.* New York: John Wiley & Sons.

O'Higgins, Micheal and John Downes. 2000. *Beating the Dow (Revised and Updated).* Collins.

Siegel, Jeremy J. 2002. *Stocks for the Long Run: The Definitive Guide to Financial Market Returns and Long-Term Investment Strategies. 4th ed.* New York: McGraw-Hill.

Index

E

economic 3, 45, 73, 81
Eli Lilly (LLY) 31
emergency fund vi, 57
energy 2, 15, 20-3, 26, 28, 32, 35-6, 41-4, 49
enterprise 1
Exelon (EXC) 28, 49
expected return 78
ExxonMobil (XOM) 2-3, 16, 21-3, 32, 36, 68

F

Facebook (FB) 23, 50-1, 57, 71-3
FB 23, 50-1, 57, 71-3
Fidelity 69
finances vii, xiii, 36, 87
financial v, ix, xi-xv, 1, 3, 7, 10, 14, 20, 22-4, 26, 31, 65, 67-70, 87
financial advisor 24, 68-9, 91
financial institution 3, 36
financial life xiii
financial literacy ix, 87
Financial literacy ix, 87
financial planner 69
financial realm xiv
financial security v, 1
financial world xi, 87
firearms viii, 80
First Niagara Financial Group (FNFG) 22-3

foreign countries 45
Fortune 500 15, 67
Foundation v, xvii, 1, 37
Fox Business 85
free trade 1, 45
Freeport-McMoRan Copper & Gold (FCX) 32
Full-brokerage firms 69
full-service brokerage account 68

G

General Electric (GE) 3, 14, 21-3, 32, 36, 48-9
General Mills (GIS) 28
General Motors (GM) 55
giving back viii, 83
global economy 39-40, 45
gold 6, 14-15, 21-3, 32-3, 43
gold. Goldcorp (GG) 15
gold stocks 15
  best 15-16, 18, 27, 33, 35, 53, 57-8, 63, 69, 72-3
Goldcorp (GG) 15
Google 14, 20, 32, 51, 72
Google (GOOG) 32, 51, 72
Greenblatt, Joel 93
growth stocks vi, 25
guide xi, xiii, 10, 71, 93
guidelines 88

H

Haliburton (HAL) 32

M

N

O

P

www.ingramcontent.com/pod-product-compliance
Lightning Source LLC
Chambersburg PA
CBHW022018170526
45157CB00003B/1277